Lyrics of a Dreamer's Heart

Lyrics of a Dreamer's Heart

FIONNA M. WRIGHT

iUniverse, Inc.
Bloomington

LYRICS OF A DREAMER'S HEART

iUniverse books may be ordered through booksellers or by contacting:

iUniverse
1663 Liberty Drive
Bloomington, IN 47403
www.iuniverse.com
1-800-Authors (1-800-288-4677)

Because of the dynamic nature of the Internet, any web addresses or links contained in this book may have changed since publication and may no longer be valid. The views expressed in this work are solely those of the author and do not necessarily reflect the views of the publisher, and the publisher hereby disclaims any responsibility for them.

Any people depicted in stock imagery provided by Thinkstock are models, and such images are being used for illustrative purposes only.
Certain stock imagery © Thinkstock.

ISBN: 978-1-4697-3537-5 (sc)
ISBN: 978-1-4697-3539-9 (hc)
ISBN: 978-1-4697-3538-2 (ebk)

Printed in the United States of America

iUniverse rev. date: 01/25/2012

For my family:
Mom, Dad, Anthony, Andre, and Aljonn,
without you, there'd be no reason.

And for my few true friends, you know who you are.
You've inspired me to make my dreams real.
Thank you forever.

I'd like to tell people stories, make them see pictures, make them cry and laugh, take them anywhere emotionally with something as deceptively simple as words.

—Michael J. Jackson

Preface

I've been on a lifelong journey to find truth, love, and beauty in every aspect of life: people, dreams, experiences, stories, relationships, and so on. I wrote this book for dreamers, for wanderers, and for anyone searching for his or her truth and purpose.

Writing has been a passion I could never escape. I can remember being just a toddler learning how to read and being fascinated with words and phonetics. I wanted to understand, to read, and to write. I'd write stories in my journals; though I didn't know the proper term then, I was compiling manuscripts. Long lost are the short stories of my youth, but the passion remains.

Throughout the years, writing has been my escape and my safe place.

Until recently, I was lost. Insecurities, doubts, and fears held me back. Since I was not formally trained in writing, I thought I could not be a writer. I was wrong. In fact, despite not being formally trained in writing, I could not stop being a writer. Writing is embedded in my soul. Words are my truth.

My hope is that, by being vulnerable and sharing my struggles and joys through this thing called life, others will benefit. If just one person gets one step closer to fulfilling his or her dreams, has a better understanding of who he or she is, or even just finds comfort in knowing he or she is not alone after reading this book, then it will have served its purpose.

Acknowledgments

Life has a funny way of making sense, even when you don't understand it. I have learned that every person I've met, every relationship in my life, every experience from the seemingly insignificant to the most significant, has had an impact on my life.

For that, I'd like to thank every person who has ever crossed my path for teaching me whatever life lesson you were supposed to teach me that somehow led me to this place.

More specifically, this book would not have been possible without my family and friends.

My mom has always been her children's biggest fan and has wholeheartedly supported any dream I tossed her way, and there have been many! Mom, your love and support have never gone unnoticed. Thank you for always letting me dream big and for truly believing in my dreams. That means the world to me, and so do you. Love you.

My dad has always been the voice of reason; his tough love instilled in me the strength I need to face the world. Though it seems like I don't hear you, Dad, I am always listening. Thank you for protecting us from the scary world growing up, but still teaching us to survive in it as adults. Love you.

My three brothers are my pride and joy, my strength, my motivation, and my backbone.

Ant: Budder, your passion and drive continue to inspire me. You've overcome some of the toughest obstacles in life, and I admire you for that. You are intelligent, strong, caring, inventive, ambitious, and loving. We are kindred spirits, which we see through our "MJ thing" so often! I'm lucky to have you as my brother. Love you.

Dre: Budder, I love you so much. You always see the beauty in life, even when others don't. You are a free spirit and are truly original, brave, charismatic, and brilliant. You still know how to make me laugh so hard that I cry, just like when we were kids. I'm lucky to be your baby sis. Don't ever give in to defeat—ever. Love you.

AJ: My baby budder, you light up my life. Our bond is unbreakable, and I swear we communicate telepathically sometimes! You are the baby of the family, yet you have an old soul; your wisdom and understanding of life are remarkable. You are one of the gentlest, most loving, most giving people ever, and also one of the most assertive, ingenious, inventive, and dynamic people ever. I'm lucky to have you as my baby brother, though you typically protect me as if I'm the baby! Love you.

This book would not have been written if it weren't for my amazing friends who, aside from keeping me half sane, encouraged and pushed me to stop being afraid and to pursue my dreams. Thank you, Alina, Ammala, Ramona, and Jasmine, for making me finally write this book! I admire each one of you for different reasons, but you are all strong, independent, enterprising, intelligent, beautiful, and ambitious. Heart you.

Changing Love

My message to the world is love.
But I was taught not to let emotions rise above.

Embedded into my soul and into my mind
was this philosophy; so sometimes into love, I go blind.

In an attempt to cleanse my heart and conscience, I loved all,
even the ones who lived to see me fall.

One person can only take so much from everyone.
Or maybe it's just that the pain outweighs the love.

The weight of everyone's problems, complaints, and cries
leaves you feeling drained, and the love you once felt dies.

Or maybe I'm just cold-hearted and the act finally vanished;
soon my loved ones will tell me I'm banished.

In tough situations in the world where I reside,
always, always having to push feelings aside.

*My mind is confused and can't tell wrong from bad or right from good . . .
Oh wait. This heart, this mind . . . misunderstood.*

*Only can tell two things: what makes me happy and what makes me sad.
But it changes in a second—and the hearts I've found are scantily clad.*

*"Mind over matter" is a routine and ritual.
It helps maintain balance while I try to stay spiritual . . .*

*Drowned in words, lost in thoughts, music, lyrics profound.
Still, tomorrow, my heart will beat to another sound.*

Constantly trapped in a heartless mind and a mindless heart.

True, love?

True love. You love. Who, love?
Me? Love see. Love he. Love she. Love me.
Why? High love. Sky love. Buy love. Good-bye, love.

Rose-Colored Glasses

With these rose-colored glasses, I see everything in red.
With a sorrowful heart, I feel everything in gray.

Love Brings

Love brings sunshine beams,
joy, and smile's gleams.
Send your love into their way,
be the one to make their day.
It will return, just believe.

Love brings wondrous prizes,
changes hearts and changes lives.
It gives hope to those in need,
heals those hearts which bleed.
Love's a magical truth to our dreams.

Beautiful Heart

What you are isn't always who you are.

*What makes someone beautiful is the heart.
What makes a heart beautiful is its pain,
understanding, accepting, growing, and
loving even more through the darkness.*

*Sometimes walking blindly through the dark
is the only way to see the light.*

Purest Love

*Worldly restrictions and judgments cannot obstruct love in its
purest form.
Searching for love in its purest form can be destructive.
Finding love in its purest form can be healing.*

Find love for all.

Soul Searching

In the darkest hours,
the loneliest times,
the emptiest heart,
with a restrained spirit
and a mystic mind—
only then do I find
my inner light,
my best friend,
my honest love,
my free spirit,
my creative mind.

Misunderstood

The purity fills your eyes
Transparent heart through your disguise
You're misunderstood by so many
Suffering judgment by them . . . and me

A people guilty of polluted thinking
Controlled your life and kept you sinking
You were raised to believe you weren't enough
Challenged so often you're filled with distrust

You were manipulated with forceful anger
And still managed to love the total stranger
You see beauty where we see ugly
Innocently loving those living corruptly

You view life beyond our capability
Escaping conformity, sometimes through hostility
Your wisdom overcomes your eccentricity
But your pain maintains your instability

Change

A journey awaits
To explore truth
Preserve youth
Cut habits loose
Accept fate

The time has come
To start fresh
Not fear death
Live on the edge
Demand freedom

Freedom of self
Freedom of mind
Freedom of eyes
Freedom of lies
Freedom some may despise

Choose to live instead
Walk the patient path ahead
Remember to not forget
Anything they said
Embrace the tears you shed

With an open heart
With burning passion
With a strong spirit
With a mission to learn
With each step firm

Desire change
Conquer pain
Never blame
Do explain
Life's game

Speak Dreams

Lost in a forest, surrounded by green and black,
Praying for someone to rescue me,
Turn to run away, but stopped by a fence.
Afar, a voice whispers, "This is your fate."
Moonlight's my only weapon against the dark;
I turn around, not knowing where,
Trying to find the path leading my heart.

People emerge, people surround me;
I am bound to each.
Heavy chains force me to the ground;
Their screams and whispers echo.
I continue walking an unfamiliar road.
Though betrayal and pain yield undeniable wrath,
There's no desire to return whence I came.

The toughest times gave me strength
The saddest times taught me appreciation
The loneliest times gave me courage
The strangest times taught me acceptance
The lovely times gave me hope
The heartbreak discovered love

Each journey forced me to grow
To be mindful of
Me, myself, you, and I.

I finally see a way out of the forest,
Strangely appears a light—a door
Behind it, my family and friends,
And understand this journey is complete.
I wake up from the dream so real,
And wonder, what did all of it mean?

Family Ties

A family torn
A family born
Painful days
Stubborn ways
Everyone prays

Smile through the lies
Try to stabilize
Love heals all
Though we still fall
Good thing we know how to crawl

Embodied in a complex
Taken out of context
A family's politics
Countless mind tricks
Still our blood runs thick

Dance Therapy

Two minds apart
A common factor in our heart
Controlled by the music
Just let go and lose it

A puppet to the dance
Don't save us from the trance
Lyrics, notes, and melodies
The purest form of therapy

Music brings no pain
And in it, we are sane
Forget the world outside
Dance together side by side

In this moment, we see eye to eye
Dancing, singing, flying high
Keep the music playing loud
Your shining light makes me proud

Pretty Girl

A beautiful tragedy for a pretty girl with a broken spirit
An enigma to herself but perfect sense to everyone else
With enough personalities to last a lifetime
For anyone who wants to hear it
Expert at living a lie equipped with credentials

I am.

I am strong, I am weak.
I am brave, I am scared.
I am outspoken, I am shy.
I am confident, I am insecure.
I am happy, I am sad.
I am dark, I am light.
I am excited, I am nervous.
I am smiling, I am crying.
I am seeking, I am hiding.
I am love, I am resentment.
I am everything, I am nothing.

Growing Pains

When she grew up, he loved her mind and her heart
But she wasn't ready to forgive and let go of the pain . . .
Then she understood and forgave
But now he loves her cautiously from a distance.

Family

The ones whose blood runs through my veins
Control every move I make . . .
The few I consider friends are there with me,
Through every step I take.

Me, More

Blinded by conformity,
Blinded by self-absorbed thinking
There's got to be more to me
Me, me, me . . .

Playing with Fire

The coldest night can't put out this fiery affair
Sweet nothings whispered and wine to ignite
Racing to the room with no time to spare
Playing under the covers all night

Romantic play-fighting 'til we both climax
No waiting to rest and catch our breath
Before giving in to passion's attack
Both aiming to please with a love to appease

This intimacy reaches deeper than all
So high on a love that's dangerous
Because of the risk involved if we fall
But it's all worth this flaming lust

Pink and Purple Flashbacks

Pink and purple flashbacks of a future past
Bright lights ignite life
See it all through broken glass
Into the beautiful mess, we dive

Memories left unbroken
A future still unspoken
Experiences illuminate
When shattered thoughts complicate

Always searching for those lights
Pink and purple gazing skies
Dream catcher, love rapture
Illuminate this future backwards

Cheers!

People come and people go
Some are friends who grew too old
Or maybe ones whose hearts turned cold
Some were only ever foes
Added to life's mysterious flow

Lessons learned hurt the most
So tonight, let's have a toast
To every pain and every laugh
That we've all ever had
Cheers! To our future, not our past

Free Spirits

My illusion was that what we had
was simple and emancipating.
In reality it was complex and destructive,
breaking laws set by society.

Free souls bound together by intimacy.
No expectations, no restrictions, no conformity,
just simple, passionate, liberating love.
Two beings on a quest for their true selves.

Enjoying the anatomy of the other along their
separate but crossing paths. And when the road split,
they parted ways and continued their journey.
A bittersweet memory is what they became.

If only it were that easy.

Pain and Pleasure

The greatest pleasure and greatest pain
come from interactions with people.
Each experience teaches a valuable lesson
from the simplest to the most complex,
from the most casual to the most intimate,
from the absolute best to the absolute worst.

No matter how hard the lesson,
something good comes from every experience.
A lesson learned and personal growth.
Energy and time is wasted dwelling on something
out of your control. Recognize the lesson to be learned
and be mindful of your ego.

Song of a Broken Heart

The overwhelming feeling of an end so near,
An end to a love once held so dear.

A love so blissful, yet so blue;
A love that was too good to be true.

Emotions and passion, kicked around like dirt,
Led us both astray, left us filled with hurt.

And now, so sadly, we approach the inevitable end,
Realizing I can't have you . . . even as my friend.

Although the feelings I have are still so strong
What we did and what we had was oh so wrong!

The love, the lust, that we swore were everlasting,
Minimized my heart to nothing and left me desperately gasping.

So badly I wanted you to be my only one for life
But for years before me, she was your wife.

Regret and heartache constantly occupy my mind,
Always wondering if true love I ever will find.

What we had was forbidden, doomed from the very start,
So now I sit writing the song of a broken heart.

Hopeless Love

Love's a drug she refuses to take
Afraid to lose it and go through withdrawal
No one copes easily with that painful mistake
She loves easily but not at all

Every broken heart leaves her shattered
After being deeply involved with love's boast
She keeps walls up to avoid death, by love so battered
Never giving in to the one she loves most

An empty life is her compromise
To dodge the hopelessness she must
Or it would only leave her to agonize
So in love she just can't trust

Prove It's True

Tell me, what is your role?
Let this mystery unfold
I don't ever do what I'm told
Refuse to be controlled
Focused, working, making my dreams real
With an image to uphold

My heart's strong but not cold
I'm wise enough to know my worth
But your smile leads me astray
Whispers from all around
But they don't make me feel afraid
Are you afraid to be betrayed?

A broken heart will make you fall
But they say time will heal it all
If you're concerned,
Don't worry—we won't fade
We'll use this love to evolve
Go together on this crusade

Fine on my own, but taking a risk
Our bond is stronger than gold
Unless there are secrets untold
Prove your word is true
That it means the world to you
That it's not a game to you

But . . . I must admit
I don't know how you'll handle it
To you I wasn't true
A mistake that I can't undo
Tell me you won't leave
Though I know you need to grieve

It was never my intention; my love for you was there
It's not a lie; I just got scared
Everything was perfect, but perfect love is rare
Refused to be hurt again, so I had an affair
Is there anything I can say? Tell me what to do
Please give us another chance and see I do love you

The act done, impossible to erase;
I've apologized so much, patiently awaiting your embrace.
If you need to move on, if you can't see this through,
Then walk away now. Our love was confused.
I couldn't trust in my head, my heart,
That you'd give honest love

Hope you understand my side;
Hope you learn to love again.
Hope you don't hurt so bad;
Hope your heart someday mends.
If only I had another chance,
I'd fix our fragile romance.

Stolen Time

Her soul was stolen
Her heart was numb
Her belly swollen
Her mind blank
But far from dumb

She had nothing left to give anymore
Every day was another pointless chore
Erratic emotions and
Dramatic acts couldn't penetrate
She'd exhausted all feelings
Aimless, no direction

Her light, her laughter, her joy
All sold for affection
Days with him passed
Then months and years too
With one question stronger than ever

Who am I? Who?
Estranged with only life in her womb
A constant reminder of a relationship entombed.
Neither strength nor love for the life growing within
Only thoughts of betrayal, loss, and sin.

The presence of her unborn child
She immediately felt
What an unlucky and cruel hand she'd been dealt.
Finally freed from the chains of an untrue love
Done with the tears and no more blues

Only to bring part of him into her world to stay
To love another him was unimaginable,
There was no way.
Emotions gone, tears still found her eyes
With striking pain, the heart cries.

Begging for forgiveness from the heavens above,
And asking the angels to shower her baby with love
That she couldn't make herself feel
No matter how hard she tried
Trying to ignore the entire ordeal.

"I'm sorry little one; please forgive me.
Don't want you to suffer from my mistake ..."
Her teary eyes doze off and she meets him in her dreams:
"Mommy, you couldn't love me;
Will sending me back set you free?"

She changes her mind, reaches to save him,
But he floats into the light.
She didn't save her baby,
A part of her history that she can't
Just rewrite.

Her life goes on as she tries to forget,
But so often she awakes drenched in sweat
From a recurring nightmare:
Being stuck in a flood,
Mortified that she's swimming in blood.

There was a time when she saw the beauty in each and every
morning.
At present, she knows no days and all of her time is spent
mourning.

No Regrets

A heart neglected
One you rejected
Yet and still,
Time not regretted

Emotions like a tidal wave
Passions kept us both enslaved
Words used as weapons
Who says we have to behave?

Knew you'd never love me so,
That one day you'd have to go
But tangled up in lust's web
Was always just enough said

So tonight, let's take it slow
I can't let my hurt show

Struggling to erase you from my mind
I wish you'd never pulled me aside

Fell for your sweet-talkin', got locked in
Held captive by my imagination,
Fairy-tale love and candy kisses
Strange sensation, this temptation

Realize this dream is my nightmare
With a broken heart left in despair
Nowhere to run, shot by love's gun
But I won't waste my cries on your love—good-bye.

Love Games

You played with my heart
You knew it from the start
A perfect love gone wrong
Now you're right where you belong

Blowing up my phone
Now you're all alone
Begging me to stay
But now it's time you pay

You're sitting in the dark
Since you tore our love apart
I'm out with my new man
A pain you just can't stand

Blame yourself for that
You won't ever get me back
See how bad it feels
When ugly truth's revealed

Royal Love

Remember when we were in control?
We were the rules, our own patrol
The world at our fingertips
Broken rules deliberate
We even commanded the star's orbit

None could steal our royalty
Our power lied in our loyalty
Our enemies didn't stand a chance
We'd melt them with one glance
Always running back to our sacred romance

Remember when our world turned cold?
We lost it all, no more gold.
A king's affair left her alone
A queen's rage had him dethroned
A kingdom's freedom snatched and sold

We lost control of everything
Divine hearts worth damaging
Sold their trust for emeralds
Greedy love forsaken
Blind love mistaken

One Soul at a Time

Being a free spirit is the only way she knows to live
Unable to stay in love, only got so much to give

Time to move on, to heal the next broken soul
One person at a time is always her goal

Sadly losing a piece of her heart each time
All of these fools lost in selfish love—a crime

Giving all she has to ease his pain
Caressing his needs so he can see past the rain

Emotions always one-sided; dreaming, hoping, wishing to be that girl
The one he fights to forget, who put his life in this pain-filled whirl

Still, she is everything he needs for the moment
Feeding him lines for her, making him the poet

Sexual healing to forget what his greed destroyed
To make him forget every second they enjoyed

Putting together the puzzle pieces that make his heart
He's ready to love her now but she's already grown apart

Drained in every aspect with her job completed
Seeing every weakness makes his love depleted

On to the next with a broken heart and burning soul
Only one person at a time is always her goal

Dream of Dreams

A dream too far but within reach
Impatiently waiting, an opportunity besieged
A burning passion that won't defuse
A mighty fire fueled by desire
This life's poetic muse

Dream Box

Box of dreams
Box of hopes
Box of wishes
Box of poems

Wish Upon a Dream

Life's surprises
Often blind us
Dreamy whispers
Into night's sky
Wake me at sunrise

Fate

Tonight's stars are
Tomorrow's fate

Dreams Beyond

Favorite dreams
Are living schemes
Where freedom rings
Beyond our existence

Chasing Dreams

Have my feet on the ground and my head in the clouds
Chasing dreams to make Momma proud
No doubts about where I'm headed
Just a hope, a dream, a wish away—
Still, sometimes I don't know where my head is,
Because dreaming is my mainstay.

Love Waits

Holding out for a love that's real
One with substance and appeal
We haven't met but our love is ideal
Both waiting for when time unveils

Our bond is stronger than unbreakable steel
With a burning passion we can't conceal
Two hearts beat time so we both yield
While we wait for this love to be unsealed

Meantime, we conquer lust's battlefield
Carefully avoiding temptation's minefield
Protecting our hearts with intuition's shield
Living for that moment when our hearts are revealed

Dream Theatre

Masked faces, so suggestive
Crying hearts, smiles that beam
Think it's time for a new perspective
Change the channel to my favorite daydream

Close my eyes to escape routine
Freedom is the only objective
Just let go, don't be apprehensive
Let's live our dream off the big screen

A dreamer's paradise
Let's run away to that lovely place
Don't analyze
Just realize this is our fate

All the possibilities
Fantasy a disease
Imaginations deceive
Beauty still believes

Take a few steps
Then catch my breath
Won't get upset but lost respect
Life gets rough

Reality is too much
Real life is just lust
But lust you can't trust, because
It usually ends in disgust

Real love is crushed
The higher you get
Means more regret
Trying to forget

A heart in debt
Dreams upon dreams
Investigating with wings
So high up but still so low

Trapped in this play
Know your role
A love you stole
Turned and sold

Just lost control
No way to console
A shattered truth, behold
Sweet mysteries untold

Deep miseries unfold
No image to uphold
No need for you to oppose
Stay if you want, or go

Consider what I propose
Sensations they can't diagnose
Feeling like an overdose
Except you won't be comatose

Passion taxed to the utmost
Already there? Almost
Must say yes, first and foremost
'Course you're the one I want the most

To delight, let's make a toast
Got me sitting here so exposed
Watching you with eyes closed
While floating on a rainbow

A yearning no one else can know
Come aboard this love boat
And live to dream this dream life,
With me

A dreamer's mind on display
Affection we can't delay
This place won't lead you astray
Lust will not betray

Lost in an embrace
While fairies dance ballet
A visionary's soufflé
A dreamer's paradise portrayed

Just One More

Trying to resist but it feels so right
This feeling is my only appetite

Pray for another day, pray for a new way
Pray for a love that heals the sting

Just can't see past the suffering
Just can't see past the high it brings

Just one more time, one more, please
Just one more love, one more tease

Staying on a temporary high to mask all lost
Attempting to escape reality at any cost

Searching for a past that was once so sweet
Now consumed with thoughts of defeat

Can't sit still, mind drifting as we speak.
Loved ones fear death, living week by week

They say, chase your dreams—but what if you live in them
Lost in thoughts, detached from all, friends with none, used by
some

Wanting to be found but refuse to stick around
Searching for a truth that was thrown out with your youth

Needing that truce for an ego that's been bruised
Looking for the proof that love isn't an excuse

Just can't see past the suffering
Just can't see past the high it brings

Just one more time, one more, please
Just one more love, one more tease

Restless

Living a life confined
Seeking a truth you can't find
Time to leave it all behind
This need cannot be defined
It is time for you to fly

Opinions, thoughts, bias, and judgment
Egos ruling, whom are we fooling?
Small minds scream the loudest
Too insecure to explore through action
Don't see how that brings satisfaction

Itching for a journey we fear
Ready to jump off of comfort's ledge
Sick of not living from the safety of our bed
A prison cell for a mind so restless
Too alive to know what rest is

Angelic

Angel, exuding light and love wherever she goes
Spreading laughter and joy to all she knows
Her light shines bright, reaching people near and far
Encouraging dreams no matter how bizarre

If I told you about her heavy heart, hidden and blue
You'd call me foolish and assume I have no clue
She floats on high with a love so pure
But unreciprocated, a broken heart with no cure

Explore

Beautiful to the core
Every man's fighting
To establish a rapport
But she's in the sky, writing.

Lost

Lost souls in control
Guilty of greed
And matching egos—
With caution, proceed.

Blessed Girl

The best girl is not the "yes" girl.
Oh yes, girl, you are blessed, girl.

Frenemies

Fabricated stories
Expert liar's masterpiece
Choose how to perceive
The friendliest enemies

Glance Back

Backwards vision protects
Against back stabs, perhaps
And violated respect
Keep going 'til you collapse

HollyWeird

Ladies and gentleman,
Emergency exits are to the left and right,
Up and down and all around.
Buckle up and hold on tight.
Don't get lost, you won't be found.
We're headed to a place where
Truth is boring, love's outdated,
Fake is real, and honesty's a lie.
Dreams come true and then destroy you.
A place where the possibilities are endless,
The sky's the limit.
Steer clear of
Empty Promises Avenue and
The Boulevard of Broken Dreams.
Lastly, to yourself be sure
To always stay true.
Welcome to HollyWeird—
Good luck!

It's Still Trickin' (If You Got It)

Droppin' bills to get laid, you trade
It's still trickin' if you sought it, applaud it
Droppin' bills to degrade, she stayed
It's still trickin' if you got it, bought it

You spend your paper though you know
You're trickin' girls who aren't whole
Who think they could be yours
Then turn around and call them hoes

Belittle them with your gold
They're easy sex, you suppose
She gets around, so you're told
Well, that makes you an asshole

But don't you know what that shows?
You're weak, not in control
Abusing power's your only goal?
Sleazy lyrics to console your ego

While smoking bowls
Claiming to be saved
Sin all night then go home and pray
Asking forgiveness for your mistakes

Leaving out how you behaved
And how much you paid
Did you pray for her to be brave?
To heal her heart and be saved?
To guide her along the way?
To show her love's not betrayed?

She's someone's baby lost in the game
You say she chose this life; you're not to blame
But trickin' girls is your claim to fame
It's still trickin' if you got it, bought it

Dear Bully: Signed, Love

Angry hearts filled with rage,
Spreading pain along their way
Souls burying their own emotional stress
By hurting others and leaving them in distress

Bullies come in many forms
They're young, old, big, small
But they all share a common goal
Of counting tears that they stole

Bullies are weak-minded
Running from their problems, misguided
They think being cool means abusing power
But picking on others makes them cowards

Bullies win a fight but lose at life
Unless they change their nasty ways
Crudely enjoying causing people harm
Catches up to them without forewarn

With karma keeping track of our every move
Bullies are bound to always lose
Their rotten behavior will no longer amuse
Misery is the only emotion accompanying abuse

Instead of ruining the lives of others
Soul search and understand your own pain
If you can conquer your own demons
You'll be preserved in love's completion

Emancipation

Trapped by the devil's schemes
Where nothing's as it seems
Rather a nightmare
Black and white versus black against white

Cold stares
Not scared
Judgment is not a right
Your delusion brought to light

The war begins
Too many battles sacrificed
Our weapons are love and knowledge
Even when you keep us out of college

We'll keep running this race
'Til color is blind, love is all we see
Distracted with sex and drugs and rap and bling
We understand this dictatorial regime

Misconstrued love we chase
"Blood, sweat, and tears"—so cliché
Except when given despite being called
Insane

About the Author

Fionna Wright, currently studying for her master's degree in multimedia communications at the Academy of Art University, has a bachelor's degree in political science from the University of California–Riverside. She has a previously published blog, Complex Thoughts. Simple Words. She was born and raised in Southern California and resides in Los Angeles, CA.